Feeling Jealous

© Aladdin Books Ltd 2008

Designed and produced by
Aladdin Books Ltd
PO Box 53987
London SW15 2SF

First published in 2008
in Great Britain
by Franklin Watts
338 Euston Road
London NW1 3BH

Franklin Watts Australia
Level 17/207 Kent Street
Sydney NSW 2000

Franklin Watts is a division of Hachette Children's Books, an Hachette Livre UK company.
www.hachettelivre.co.uk

ISBN 978 0 7496 7502 8

A catalogue record for
this book is available
from the British Library.

Illustrator: Christopher O'Neill

The author, Sarah Levete, has written and edited many books for young people
on social issues and other topics.

Dewey Classification:
152.4'8

Printed in China

Feeling Jealous

Sarah Levete

Aladdin/Watts

London • Sydney

Contents

Introduction

These children go to the same school. They have all felt jealous of other people or their belongings. Some of them also know what it feels like when someone is jealous of them. Have you ever felt jealous? Join these friends and other children as they discuss their feelings.

Being jealous can make you unkind to the people you love.

I was jealous of my brother. It made me feel lonely.

It's upsetting if someone is jealous of you.

Everyone is different and has different belongings.

Jealousy can make you fed up with the things you have.

What Is Jealousy?

Grace and Megan always walk to school together. Today, Grace is in a bad mood. She is jealous because her friend, Oona, has got some new clothes. Megan used to be jealous of her brother, Sam. She thought her mum loved Sam more than her. Jealousy is a feeling that what someone else has, or does, is better than what you have, or do.

You may feel jealous just for a moment or for a long time.

I used to be jealous of my brother. I thought he was Mum's favourite.

I'm really jealous of Oona. She's always got new things.

6

▶ Jealous About People

Have you ever felt cross with a person because he or she is good at something? This is feeling jealous about a person. It can make you think that no one takes any notice of you or that you are less special than the other person.

◀ Jealous About Things

Some people feel jealous of other's belongings. They may worry that what they have will be taken away from them. People who feel jealous like this can find it hard to share their toys and games.

▶ Jealous Of You

Do you have an older or younger brother or sister who is jealous of you? It can be difficult when someone else is jealous of you – you may feel as if you have done something wrong,

Megan, why were you jealous of your brother, Sam?
"Sam was allowed to do all the things I wasn't allowed to do.
Even when he was naughty, nobody ever got cross with him.
I never had new clothes. I always used to have his old things."

Jealous About Belongings

Alex and Charlie are out cycling, but Charlie is in a bad mood. His mum won't buy him a new pair of trainers like his brother's. Alex thinks Charlie is being silly – he's already got a great pair of trainers! Have you ever wanted something you couldn't have? How did it make you feel?

Do you feel happy for your friends… or jealous of what they have?

It's not fair. Mum won't let me have new trainers like my big brother's.

Why do you want new trainers? What's wrong with yours?

Story: What About Me?

1 Tom was given a computer game for his birthday. He really liked it.

2 Two days later, Tom's friend, Pete, was given a different game.

> It's not fair. I wanted a game like Pete's. It's much better than mine.

3 Tom went home feeling very angry. He now wanted Pete's present.

Why did Tom behave like this?

Tom decided that Pete's game was better than his own. Tom's jealousy stopped him from enjoying his own game. It made Tom say unkind things to his parents. If Tom had played with his own game and asked Pete if he would like to play with it too, Pete may have let Tom have a go on his game.

▶ Why Can't I Have?

Some people have more than others. This may feel unfair. You may sometimes want what someone else has. Try not to let this make you mean towards a person or make you say hurtful things. That won't change the situation.

Why can't we have a house and garden like hers?

▼ Pleased Or Cross?

Feeling jealous can make you believe what someone else has is always better than what you have, even if it is exactly the same!

Why not try to enjoy those things which you do have instead of wishing you had someone else's belongings. Do you still feel as jealous?

Story: I Want It Now!

1 Tom and Emma were both given new toys. Tom wanted to play with Emma's present.

2 Emma agreed and let Tom play with her car-racing set.

3 As soon as Tom saw that Emma was happy with his skateboard, he wanted it back.

Why does Tom always want what Emma has got?

Tom is jealous that Emma can play happily with whatever she has. Even if Tom had the best game or toy in the world, he would still want to play with what Emma had. If Tom stopped feeling jealous about what Emma was doing, he would be able to have fun with his toys, too.

Chris, do you ever feel jealous?
"Sometimes I wish I had some of the things my friends have.
But usually they let me play with their toys. There's no point in
feeling jealous – you forget what good things you do have."

Jealous About People

During break-time at school, Janice is telling her best friend, Phoebe, that she doesn't like Matt. Matt recently joined the school. Janice is jealous because Matt is now friends with Phoebe as well. Phoebe doesn't understand why all three of them can't be friends.
Have you ever felt jealous in this way?

Jealousy can be about looks.

I wish Matt had gone to another school.

Why? I think he's really friendly.

It's not fair. She's my best friend.

 ## Friends

If you are best friends with someone and he or she becomes friends with someone else you may feel jealous and no longer special. Best friends are great, but you can have other types of friends as well. The best kinds of friends are the friends you can share.

◀ Parents

If you live with one parent, it can be difficult to get used to that parent having a new partner or a special friend. But just because your mum or dad spends some time with a new partner, it doesn't mean that he or she doesn't still love you.

▶ Brothers And Sisters

It can make you feel jealous if you think that your parents pay more attention to your brother or sister. Each person in a family is different. Sometimes one child will need lots of attention. At other times, you may get more attention. Talk to your parents about how you feel.

Why does she always get the attention?

Story: A Rude Reply

1 Jane didn't like Neeta. Neeta always did well at school and was picked as team captain.

2 Neeta asked Jane if she wanted to be in her team.

> Come on, play with us.

> Why would I want to be in your team?

3 Jane was rude to Neeta and said she wouldn't be in her team.

Why was Jane rude to Neeta?

Jane was jealous that Neeta did well at school and had lots of friends. But by being rude to Neeta, Jane lost out on the chance to be in the team and to get to know Neeta and her friends. Jane's classmates thought she was very rude, so her jealousy made things even more difficult.

▶ Feeling Lonely Or Left Out

If you feel shy, you may be jealous of someone else who has lots of friends. But feeling jealous won't make it easier to make friends – it can make it more difficult! Everyone can feel left out sometimes. If you see someone who looks a bit lonely, why not make a special effort to be nice to them?

▼ Everyone Is Different

That's what makes the world interesting. Not everyone is good at everything. But if you try your best at whatever you are doing, then there is no reason to feel jealous. Try to remember that what you do is just as important as what someone else is doing.

Phoebe, do you get jealous of people?

"I used to be jealous of a girl in my school who was good at everything. It made me feel like I was hopeless. But when I talked to my mum she helped me understand that I was good at lots of things, too. After that I became friends with the other girl."

Jealousy Can Make You...

Last week Paddy refused to go to Jack's birthday party. Jack was really upset. He couldn't understand why Paddy was being unfriendly. Now Paddy realises he was unfair. He is explaining to Jack that he felt jealous. Feeling jealous can make you upset the people you care about.

You may feel very cross.

Why didn't you want to come to my party?

I wanted to make you feel sorry for having a new friend apart from me.

You may miss out on good things.

19

▶ Spoil Sport

Sometimes you may feel so jealous that you want to spoil what someone else has. But ruining someone else's things won't make you feel better. It could even get you into serious trouble. Tell a grown-up about how you feel.

I could tear up her picture...

...or I could tell Dad how I feel.

◀ Sad Feelings

Jealousy can make you feel lots of different things. It can make you angry or lonely. It can make you forget what is good. It is hard to be happy if you spend too much time worrying about what other people do or have.

▶ No Fun To Be With

Jealousy can make you feel mean and unkind. This can make it difficult to be friendly. It can make it hard for other people to be friends with you.

20

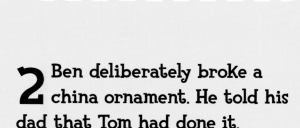

Tom, you did really well in sport this term.

Jealousy Can Make You...

Story: Blaming Tom

1 Ben was jealous of his younger brother, Tom, who always did well at school.

Tom did it, not me.

2 Ben deliberately broke a china ornament. He told his dad that Tom had done it.

3 Tom denied it. Their dad was cross with both of them.

Why did Ben want to get Tom into trouble?

Ben was jealous of Tom. He wanted their dad to stop thinking that Tom was so good. But getting Tom into trouble didn't make Ben's jealousy go away. It would have been better if Ben had talked to his dad about his feelings, even if his dad disagreed with him.

▶ Feeling Cross

Feeling jealous will only make you feel unhappy with everything you have. It can make you dislike your own toys. It can make you cross with the people you love.

▼ Try Talking

If you feel that someone else gets more attention than you, try talking to a grown-up you trust. The grown-up may not agree with your point of view and the situation may not change, but talking can help the way you feel.

Paddy, are you still feeling jealous?
"A bit, but I know it's not fair, and being jealous
nearly lost me my best friend. I upset Jack and I was
unfair to his new friend, Omar, too. Now, the three of
us go round together."

Jealous About You?

Aaliyah is asking her friend Zara about school. Zara says she's enjoying it now, but she was unhappy at first: one of the girls was jealous of her because she was a good dancer. Talking to her mum made Zara realise she hadn't done anything wrong. It can be really upsetting when someone is jealous of you.

You may feel confused.
You may feel upset.

It's horrible when someone is jealous of you.

Yeah. It makes you feel as if you have done something wrong.

Jealous About You?

▶ Be Friendly

People who are jealous will also be feeling unhappy. Make them feel a bit special. Ask if they want to play with you or with your toys. It is unkind and unfair to show off or brag about what you have.

Do you want to play with us?

◀ Speak Up

Sometimes a person may feel so jealous that he or she will do mean things. If someone is bullying you, such as saying nasty things, hitting you or taking things from you, tell a grown-up you trust such as your mum, dad, or teacher.

Zara, how did you feel when your classmate was jealous of you?

"At first, I thought I had done something to upset her. She was really unfriendly to me. Then one of the other girls told me she was just jealous. Talking to Mum about it made me feel better."

How To Stop Feeling Jealous

Being jealous can make you miss out on good friendships. Paddy stopped feeling jealous when he realised that he was being unfair, and that Jack wouldn't want to be his friend any more. He also realised that Jack's new friend, Omar, could be his friend too.

It can be good to share.

I realised that there was no point in being jealous. I still want us to be mates.

Omar's great, but you're still my friend.

▶ **Put It On Paper**

A feeling of jealousy can pass very quickly. If it doesn't, try talking to a grown-up or an elder brother or sister. Sometimes it helps to get rid of the feeling by drawing a picture or writing down how you feel.

◀ **Everyone's Special**

Remember that the world is made up of lots of different people. Everyone is special and everyone is different. We all have different belongings. We all have things we are good at, and we all have things we are not so good at.

Grace, do you still feel jealous of your friends?

"If I feel jealous about my friends' new clothes or shoes, I write down how I feel instead of getting cross with them. It helps make the feelings go away. It's much nicer when you don't feel jealous."

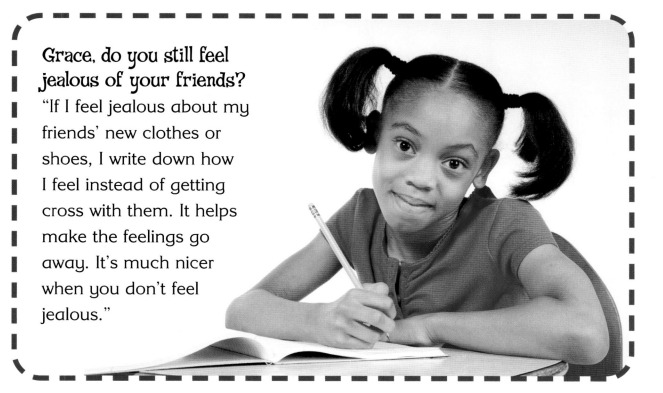

Don't Forget...

1

How do you feel now you are all friends, Paddy?

"It's great. Sometimes, we go round together and sometimes we don't. Friends are brilliant, but it's OK to be on your own, too."

What do you think about jealousy, Jack? "Jealousy makes everyone feel horrible. It's always worth trying to sort it out. Otherwise everyone gets hurt."

2

How do you feel now, Phoebe?

"Sometimes I still get jealous at other people who are better at sport than me. But I realise that everyone's different and I've learned to enjoy the things I'm good at rather than worrying about everyone else."

3

What can you do if someone is jealous of you, Zara?

"Try not to let it upset you. If the person is spoiling your things or saying mean things to you, tell your parents or a teacher. If you do have more things than someone else, don't show off – that's really unfair."

4

What can you do to stop feeling jealous, Grace?

"Talk about your feelings – being jealous is no fun. Remember the things that you do have and enjoy them. And remember that friends are more important than anything else."

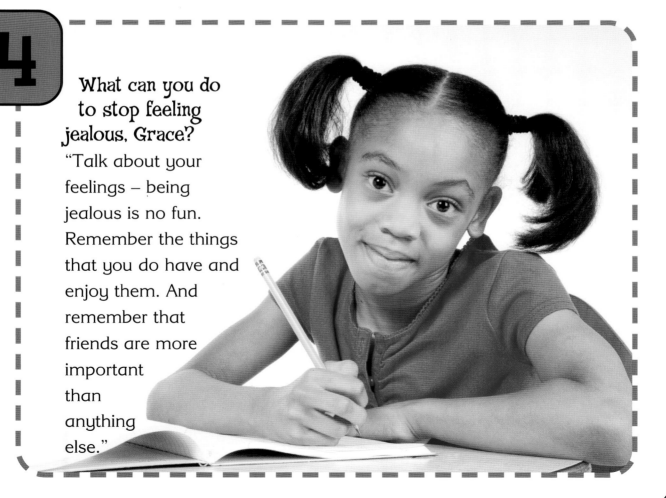

Find Out More About Dealing With Jealous Feelings

Helpful Addresses and Phone Numbers

Talking about problems or worries can really help. If you can't talk to someone close to you, then try ringing one of these organisations:

Childline
Tel: 0800 1111
A 24-hour free helpline for children. The number won't show up on a telephone bill if you ring them.

Kids Helpline, Australia
Tel: 1800 55 1800
A 24-hour free helpline for children. Also online help: www.kidshelp.com.au

NSPCC (National Society for the Prevention of Cruelty to Children)
Tel: 0808 800 500
Asian helpline: 0800 096 7719
A 24-hour free helpline offering counselling and practical advice for young people.

Parentline Plus
Tel: 0808 800 2222
A 24-hour free helpline offering counselling and support to parents on many issues, including dealing with sibling rivalry.

On the Web

These websites are also helpful. You can get in touch with some of them using email:

www.nspcc.org.uk

www.kidshelp.com.au

www.kidshealth.org/kid/

www.pbskids.org/itsmylife/family/
sibrivalry

www.parentlineplus.org.uk

www.parentlink.act.gov.au/
parenting guides

Further Reading

If you want to read more about dealing with jealous feelings, try:

Thoughts and Feelings: Our Stepfamily by Julie Johnson (Aladdin/Watts)

Thoughts and Feelings: Our New Baby by Jen Green (Aladdin/Watts)

Not Like I'm Jealous or Anything by Marissa Walsh (Delacorte Books)

Jealous by Janine Amos (Cherrytree Books)

Bratty Brothers and Selfish Sisters by R.W. Alley (One Caring Place)

Oh Brother… Oh Sister: A Sister's Guide to Getting Along by Brooks Whitney (American Girl Library)

Index

Photocredits

All photos from istockphoto.com except 13, 24, 25, 29 top – Corbis.

All the photos in this book have been posed by models.